HANUMAN

a story from Ramayana

Story and pictures by Biman Mullick

Once upon a time in India there lived a Prince called Rama and his beautiful wife, Sita.

2

On the island of Lanka there lived a ten-headed demon King called Ravana. One day Ravana went to India and stole Sita. He hid her in his palace garden.

Rama and his army of monkey soldiers went to rescue Sita. They went to war with the demon King Ravana.

During the war Prince Rama's brother, Prince Lakshmana, was badly hurt and made unconscious by a poisoned arrow. Prince Lakshmana needed a doctor.

5

The Royal Doctor was brought to examine Prince Lakshmana. 'I'll need a very rare herb called Vishalyakarani to make the Prince better. But it only grows on top of the mountain Gandhamadan in India,' said the doctor.

'I will fetch it for you,' said Hanuman, the monkey General.
'You must bring it to me before sunrise,' said the doctor, 'or the medicine will not work.'

Hanuman did not waste time and set off at midnight. He used his magic powers to help him make a giant leap across the ocean and he landed on the mountain Gandhamadan.

In the light of the moon, Hanuman searched all over the mountain looking for the herb Vishalyakarani. He found lots of other herbs but not this special one.

Hanuman was very worried because he knew in a few hours the sun would rise and then it would be too late.

To save time Hanuman used his magic powers again. This time he made himself nearly as big as the mountain. He pulled up the whole mountain, took it on his hand and, making another huge leap, rose high up into the sky.

To his horror on his way to Lanka, he noticed the sun was about to rise in the east. Hanuman changed direction and flew to the rising sun. He made himself bigger than before, and put the sun under his arm.

'Let me go, let me go!' cried the angry sun. Hanuman took no notice. Holding the mountain Gandhamadan in one hand and keeping the sun under his arm, he turned and flew on.

When he landed back on the island Hanuman put the mountain down in front of the Royal Doctor. The doctor took a long time to find the special herb. Eventually he found it and used it to help Prince Lakshmana.

The sun was still under Hanuman's arm. It was struggling to shine and kept screaming, 'Let me go, let me go!'

'I will not let you go until Prince Lakshmana is better,' said Hanuman.

Suddenly the Prince opened his eyes and got up.
Everyone was delighted. Hanuman let the sun go
and it shot up into the sky.

With the help of Hanuman and his monkey
soldiers, Rama went on to rescue Sita.

But that's another story!